Table of Contents

INTRODUCTION TO BLOCKCHAIN 2
    WHAT IS A BLOCKCHAIN 5

BLOCKCHAIN DIAGRAM 7

HISTORY OF BLOCKCHAIN 12
    SATASHI NAKAMOTO 12

BITCOIN REVOLUTION 15
    WHY WAS BITCOIN CREATED? 17
    EVOLUTION OF BITCOIN 26
        People and Dates *26*

ALTCOINS 37

MINING EXPLAINED 46

SMART CONTRACTS 50

BLOCKCHAIN FACTS SUMMARIZED 52

CLOSING 56

BITCOIN QUOTES 59

RESOURCES 64

COPYRIGHT 65

Introduction to Blockchain

I wanted to write this book because like most people, I'm sure you're hearing, reading, or watching something which talks about Blockchain, Bitcoin and/or Cryptocurrency. The reason for the recent press is due to the volatility of the cryptocurrency market, specifically Bitcoin. I'll explain first what a blockchain is, then dive into Bitcoin and other coin descriptions (Altcoins).

Before continuing, you may be wondering what a cryptocurrency is. The formal definition is, a digital currency in which encryption techniques are used to regulate the generation of units of currency and verify the transfer of funds, operating independently of a central bank. The "independently of a central bank" is key to the whole technology and recent press since it involves blockchain/decentralization which I'll reference later in the book.

In addition, I'll list out some of the key players and dates involved with the creation of cryptocurrencies, and wrap up with some famous recent quotes by high profile people. This book is not intended to be on advise or investment strategy, but more of an information resource so you can be better informed. The more you learn about this technology, the better you'll be prepared in the coming years.

Blockchain was first created in 1991, but was not really adopted or used until Satoshi Nakamoto in 2009. He used this technology to create the digital cryptocurrency, Bitcoin.

Big business is now getting involved with blockchain technology. IBM and Microsoft have spent millions and are building cloud infrastructures for their customers as early adopters. As an example, food manufacturers can set up their own food safety network and the medical industry is researching ways for identify management, medical, and insurance records in their own blockchain. Banks and financial institutions are investing huge amounts of money in research into ways they can adopt and utilize this new technology.

If there's anything which has digital transactions, then blockchain is a viable solution. There will be numerous roadblocks and hurdles before blockchain becomes fully adopted. Regulatory and government oversight are inevitable, but one thing is certain, blockchain is here to stay and is the next biggest technical innovation in our lifetime.

What is a Blockchain

In essence, a blockchain is a distributed, decentralized ledger or database which stores shared data in "blocks". These blocks are encrypted and store historical information of each block before it and are chained together. The blockchain consists of 2 main components, the decentralized network and the ledger or database itself. It is open source and everyone can see the ledger but cannot see the contents because of it's encryption. In a couple pages is a high level diagram which shows the path of an initial transaction request, the creation of blocks to be added to a chain, and some potential uses or applications of blockchain technology.

The book, Blockchain Revolution: How the Technology Behind Bitcoin Is Changing Money, Business, and the World, explains the Bitcoin model:

"Bitcoin or other digital currency isn't saved in a file somewhere; it's represented by transactions recorded in a blockchain—kind of like a global spreadsheet or ledger, which leverages the resources of a large P2P network to verify and approve each Bitcoin transaction. Each blockchain, like the [Bitcoin blockchain] is distributed: it runs on computers provided by volunteers around the world. There is no central database to hack. The blockchain is public: anyone can view it at any time because it resides on the network... and the blockchain is encrypted... it uses public and private keys (rather like a two-key system to access a safety deposit box) to maintain virtual security. This new digital ledger can be programmed to record virtually everything of value and importance to humankind: birth and death certificates, marriage licenses, deeds and titles of ownership, educational degrees, financial accounts, medical procedures, insurance claims, votes, provenance of food, or anything else that can be expressed in code."

Blockchain Diagram

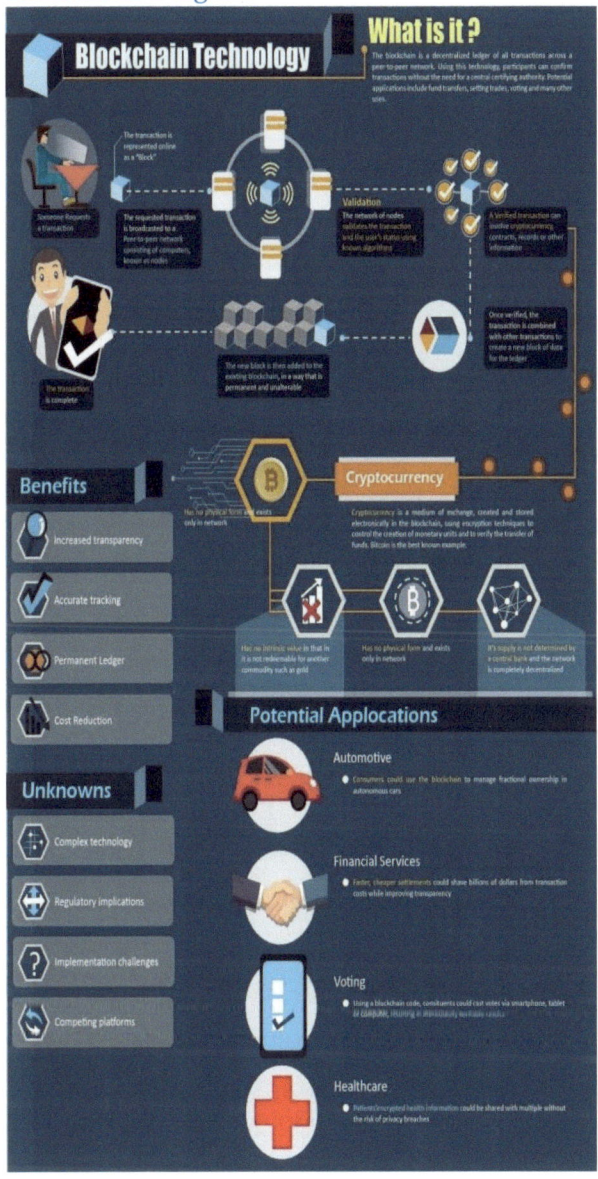

Blockchains have properties such that once data has been recorded, it is nearly impossible to change it. Each block contains some data, the hash (think of as an identifier, or fingerprint) and the hash of the previous block. The data stored inside a block depends on what type of blockchain it is.

For example, the Bitcoin blockchain contains information of a transaction, such as the hash (again, an identifier), sender, receiver, and amount of coins. Once a block is created, it's hash is calculated.

Changing something inside the block will cause the hash to change. Hashes are beneficial in order to detect any changes to blocks. If the hash, or identifier, of the block changes it is not technically considered the same block.

This goes on and on, and what you have is a chain of blocks, hence the term - Blockchain.

The linking of blocks through unique identifiers, or hashes, is what makes the blockchain so secure. Since each block has a hash, or identifier, these all link or chain back up to an original block. This 1st block is called the "Genesis" block. You can have blockchains specifically for each industry it's supporting. For example, Bitcoin has it's own blockchain, as do other cryptocurrencies. Hospital, banks, mortgage companies can have their own as well. You name it, and a blockchain can be setup on it's behalf.

If, for example, someone hacks and tampers into any block within the chain, this causes the hash to change. If that happens, technically that makes all the subsequent blocks invalid. The algorithms and computational power of the blockchain prevents this type of attack by recalculating through other hashes and builds that block again.

To minimize this risk, blockchains have something called "Proof-of-work". Proof of work is a protocol which basically slows down the creation of new blocks. It takes Bitcoin about 10 minutes to run the calculation for a required "proof of work". Once the proof of work if verified by the network, a new block is added to the chain. This ingenuity ensures the security and makes it virtually impossible to tamper or alter blocks.

Basically, if you tamper with a block, you'll need to recalculate all the "proof of work" for all subsequent blocks, and since there's an in-built delay, it would take an inordinate amount of time. The secure features of blockchain are not only due to the hashes and Proof of Work previously mentioned, but also by being distributed via peer to peer.

There is no central authority, like a bank or institution, to monitor the chain. Instead, blockchains are distributed and decentralized utilizing this peer-to-peer network, where anyone is allowed to join.

When someone joins this network, they get access and a copy of the blockchain. So again, when someone creates a new block, everyone on the network through each node verifies the block to ensure it hasn't been altered or tampered with. If everything validates, then each node adds blocks to their chain and this, in turn, creates **consensus** amongst the peer to peer network. The machines connected to this node and associated blockchain will reject any blocks that have been tampered with as well as other nodes in the network.

In order for a tamper or hack of all blocks to work, the proof of work would have to be redone, and they would have to control greater than 50 percent of the network. This network can be considered a **"trustless system"**, but it actually serves to build a system of trust. Since the blockchain verifies each transaction through Proof of Work, no trust is needed between parties.

The Proof of work comes from miners as they put the blocks together. We will discuss mining in a later section, but essentially the miners verify transactions which get added to the ledger or blockchain. Blockchain to digital transactions is similar to how the internet is for communication. Years ago the internet formed a small set of networks and was unknown to most people. Gradually, people started exploring the internet and today has formed a huge chain of people exchanging information across geographically different locations. Similarly, blockchain can be visualized as a growing chain of blocks, essentially maintained to trigger digital transactions.

History of Blockchain

The history of blockchain is traced back to the early 1990's where W. Scott Stornetta and Stuart Haber in 1991, described the first work around defining cryptographically secure chain of blocks. After this, there were several research efforts around blockchain by Bayer, Stornetta and Haber. In 1992, a variant of blockchain with Merkel Trees Inc. was introduced to improve efficiency and effectively collect several documents into a single block.

Satashi Nakamoto

In 2008, with all this research underway, the first distributed blockchain was documented and conceptualized by an anonymous person named "Satoshi Nakamoto". No one knows to this day who Satoshi Nakamoto is, or if the name is a group of developers.

Following this, in 2009, the first ever blockchain implementation was made for digital currency, called "Bitcoin". This was around the period, when the world was battling a major financial crisis, following the market crash in September 2008 and the economy downfall in 2008-2009 where almost 15 banks in the United States failed. Several banks and financial authorities wanted to explore newer trends and bitcoins opened newer ventures for digital transactions.

Blockchain works as a public ledger for all transactions. Rapid progress around blockchain and bitcoin was made around 2008-2010. The first white paper published in the name of Satoshi Nakamoto can be seen at - https://bitcoin.org/bitcoin.pdf. In 2009, this was implemented as open source software.

Until 2010, Satoshi Nakamoto continued collaborating with several open source developers on Bitcoin. There are several different theories behind the identity of Satoshi Nakamoto, none of which have any substantial evidence. Regardless, the entire concept and implementation of blockchain has gained significant recognition throughout the cyberspace market, news, financial sector, and has achieved several key milestones.

Blockchain has gained higher levels of maturity and is still evolving. It has brought a new vision around cyberspace and solved many issues around cryptographically securing digital payments. Blockchain easily allows strangers to exchange value in cyberspace. Apart from bitcoin, there are several potential markets and domains which are being evaluated to incorporate blockchain. By 2014, there were more than 80 uses of blockchain which have been documented. After 2014, newer applications incorporating blockchain are commonly referred as "Blockchain 2.0".

Bitcoin Revolution

Bitcoin is the first ever introduced "cryptocurrency" developed for worldwide, distributed payment systems. Bitcoins are used as digital currency and is the first ever cryptocurrency. Bitcoins have gained immense popularity and are most used by almost every cryptocurrency exchanges. There has also been a lot of controversy surrounding the concept of Bitcoin and other cryptocurrencies. This "virtual money" has no tangible value and is not backed by anything. The prices are extremely volatile and the value is based solely on supply and demand.

This is true, but if you think the dollar is any safer think of the following. If just 10% of the population were to request withdrawal of their money from banks, the entire banking industry would fold. The banks do not store your cash per se, but rather invest it for profit. If the US government needs to fund something and is not based on balancing their budgets, they just print more money. Bitcoin and other cryptocurrencies are different in there is only a maximum number of currency ever generated and is capped. It is an inflation hedger since printing of money by the government results in inflation. As more exchanges start trading Bitcoin and other virtual currency, it will legitimize this new currency. Most recently, the Chicago Board Options Exchange began offering Bitcoin futures. There is some discussion of including in Nasdaq potentially in 2018 as well.

Bitcoin transactions are made over a peer to peer network, directly between two entities without interference of any third party, and are secured through cryptography. So then you ask, "what is cryptography". The simple definition is: Cryptography is a method of storing and transmitting data in a particular form so that only those for whom it is intended can read and process it.

Why was Bitcoin created?

Throughout history there have been numerous problems with the central banking industry. Most recently and notably was the housing crisis in the 2000's. Bitcoin was created as a digital currency which would potentially eliminate all the problems we have for paying things online. While we think the system we have in place may be reasonable and good since it technically works, everything that we buy has to go through a bank, credit card company, or financial institution. They, in turn, take a cut from every transaction and they rely on our "trust".

You have to trust the banks with your security and trust they keep your details safe. There have been numerous attempts at eliminating the middleman or banks and to work out a payment system. The problem is how do you prove that you've paid for something or verify that you actually do have the money to spend. As mentioned earlier, in 2008 an anonymous programmer with the name, "Satoshi Nakamoto" wrote a paper on a cryptography blog which proposed a solution to these and other problems. He proposed rather than using a bank, credit card, or financial institution of recording and storing transactions in their own ledger, all users would record their transactions to a fully decentralized ledger or database online where everyone has access to it. This environment online is the basis for the blockchain as explained earlier. It would be much more secure, faster, and cheaper since it eliminates the need for banks. It was created as a revolution against big banks due to the corruption and greed associated with the mortgage crisis and bank bailout. This is why Satoshi Nagamoto, with obvious sarcasm, named the genesis block on the Bitcoin blockchain, "**"03/Jan/2009 Chancellor on brink of second bailout for banks**".

As mentioned you would have the ability to instantaneously send money anywhere in the world, again – more secure, faster, and cheaper. This is the reason big banks don't want this done in a silo or at all. US banks have invested millions in research to develop their own blockchain to contain assets and keep the currency to dollars. As a result of the recent intense publicity, it has drawn sharp criticism by big banks, as this model will take away the need for their current operating model. Their fear is that everyone or essentially their own cellphones would be their own bank. It would certainly be a major market disruptor and make us all think about how we store, secure, and transfer currency.

Bitcoins are created as a reward for a process called mining and for the most part, can be exchanged for other currencies. Mining is the record keeping of these transitions, which are done with significant computer processing power. A person involved in the process of mining is called a "miner". A miner is responsible for keeping the blockchain consistent and unalterable by repeatedly verifying the broadcast transitions and adding blocks to the existing chain of records.

As a proof of work, the bitcoin miner has to find a number called "nonce". In terms of cryptography, a nonce is an arbitrary number which can be used only once, hence the name, "nonce" number only once. This is a random or pseudo random number which is used in any authentication protocol. The discovered nonce has to be used along with the block hashed content. Hashed block content along with nonce should result in a numeric value which is smaller than the network's difficulty target.

The complete bitcoin network has a set value of a global difficulty target. To be accepted in the network, any new block created by a bitcoin miner has to have a numeric value lesser than this difficulty target. As a general rule of thumb, proof of work is easily verified by anyone on the network. However, generating the proof of work is a time consuming process and requires trials with different nonce values. The difficulty level for the network is adjusted based on the network's latest performance. The average time between new blocks creation is about at 10 minutes. Studies show that between March 2014 and March 2015, for the one-year duration, the average number of nonces a miner had to try before arriving at a new block increased from 16.4 quintillion to 200 quintillion.

As mentioned previously, the whole concept of implementing proof of work along with chain of blocks makes the entire network secure and hard to modify.

A modification to the block has to be accepted by the entire network, thereby making it almost impossible for any attacker to make any arbitrary modifications. As the network grows and new blocks are added, the difficulty of modifying the blocks increases.

So what incentive does a miner have? A successful miner will receive a reward for the new blocks. After creating a new block, the miner gets the newly created Bitcoins along with the transaction fees. As of July 2016, the reward amounted to 12.5 newly formed Bitcoins per block, which was added to the blockchain. In order to claim the reward on successful mining, a special transaction called coinbase is included as part of the payment process.

Each and every new bitcoin is created in these coinbase transactions. Currently the limit is set to a maximum of 21 million bitcoins ever generated. The bitcoin protocol specifies that the reward will be halved in every four years. Eventually the reward will be reduced to zero once the limit of 21 million bitcoins is reached. After this the record keeping will be solely rewarded by transaction fees with no additional rewards.

The limit of 21 million was arrived at by the creator of bitcoins Satoshi Nakamoto. It is estimated that the rate of generation of bitcoins will be halved in every four years until all are in circulation. An important concept around Bitcoin and blockchain is the "wallet". All information required for bitcoin transactions, are placed in a virtual wallet. Bitcoins are inseparable from the blockchain public ledger; however, all the related information is placed in the wallet. It basically stores the digital credentials of one's Bitcoin holdings. As mentioned, Bitcoin uses public key cryptography. A wallet is a collection of these public and private keys. There are different types of wallets such as Sofware wallets, online wallets, physical wallets, hardware wallets, paper wallets. Software wallets not only are responsible for holding credentials, but also allow spending of Bitcoins. Software wallets are further classified as lightweight clients and full clients. Full client requires keeping the full local copy of the blockchain. Full clients are the most reliable and secure way of using the network. The challenge in full client is the size and complexity. In contrast, lightweight clients do not require to keep the complete blockchain local copy. Lightweight clients are much faster in transaction time and require least computation. However, in case of lightweight clients, the user must trust the server. In both software wallets, the onus of keeping the private key secure, lies with the user. Online wallets make use of a Wallet provider and requires the user to trust the online wallet provider. Physical wallets store credentials offline and paper wallets are paper printouts with the required credentials. Hardware wallets store credentials offline, while facilitating transactions.

In theory, Bitcoin could replace physical currency, however virtual currency depends heavily on the current market value and a sudden crash can result in making bitcoins almost worthless based on volatility and still relatively new technology. Currently, there are more than 15 million Bitcoins in circulation over the complete transaction chain. As of this writing, each Bitcoin is roughly around $16,000, which makes it highly visible to speculative investors and an extremely high risk investment.

Until the price stabilizes, much like a commodity as gold or silver, the proposition of replacing physical currency is limited. It is believed that as a creator, Satoshi Nakamoto owns millions of such bitcoins and if he were to sell a small amount, it would result in investors selling their own Bitcoin and could result in a major correction in value. The value is currently solely based on supply and demand, and is not based on anything else of value.

For example, our dollar was once based against the value of gold, and subsequently is now back by the Federal Reserve or US Government. This is where a lot of controversy around valuating Bitcoin comes into play, as there is no comparable valuation.

To summarize, Bitcoin is pseudonymous. Pseudonymous means the funds are not tied back to the real world but are linked to Bitcoin addresses. Sending and receiving Bitcoins is similar to writing under a pseudonym. It may not be feasible to identify every owner of bitcoin address, however, all transactions over the blockchain are public yet private. This has caused a lot of controversy in the public sector as governments, agencies, law enforcement cannot track down the sender and receiver of transactions because of the secure technology built into the blockchain.

This is as per design suggested by Satoshi Nakamoto in his whitepaper, where he recommended use of new address for every transaction to avoid getting linked to a common owner. This is similar to writing several books under different pseudonyms. Basically, your transactions are anonymous to the network, but the decentralized network encrypts, secures, and ensures trust in the transaction, even though we don't inherently trust each other. I know, sounds Zen like, but that's what makes this technology so revolutionary.

Evolution of Bitcoin

People and Dates

This section includes major transformation, dates, and people involved with the evolution of Bitcoin. Prior to Bitcoins, there were several other digital cash technologies such as the Ecash protocol developed by Stefan Brands and David Chaum. Other technologies include Hashcash developed by Adam Back which also incorporated proof of work concept. Distributed digital cryptocurrencies, was first introduced in b-money developed by Wei Dai which was followed by Nick Szabo's bit gold. Reusable Proof of Work was developed by Hal Finney, using Hashcash as its proof of work algorithm.

On August 18th, 2008, bitcoin.org domain was registered. In the same year, on October 31st 2008 Satoshi Nakamoto wrote the first white paper. The link to the white paper was published and authored by Satoshi Nakamoto with the title "Bitcoin: A peer to peer Electronic cash system". Bitcoins were first introduced in January 2009 by Satoshi Nakamoto and led to the existence of the bitcoin chain and bitcoin network worldwide. Satoshi Nakamoto was the first to mine the Bitcoins and was awarded 50 bitcoins. The coinbase of the block had the text "The Times 03 Jan 2009 Chancellor on brink of second bailout for banks".

One of the early adopters of bitcoins was Hal Finney. The first ever bitcoin transaction was made between Satoshi Nakamoto and Hal Finney, where Hal Finney received 10 bitcoins from Satoshi Nakamoto. Hal Finney downloaded the bitcoin software on the same day as the launch of bitcoin network.

Other supporters of bitcoin, includes Wei Dai creator of b-money and Nick Szabo creator of bit gold. In 2010, Nakamoto stepped back and handed the network alert key to Gavin Andresen, who became the lead developer at Bitcoin Foundation. Bitcoin Foundation is a bitcoin driven community support.

It is estimated that, in the early days Satoshi Nakamoto mined almost 1 million Bitcoins. The value of first bitcoin transaction was negotiated on the bitcoin forum. One of the most notable transactions during that early time was 10,000 Bitcoin used to purchase two pizzas from Papa John's.

A major vulnerability in the bitcoin protocol was exposed on August 6th, 2010. This vulnerability resulted in transactions not being properly verified and still to be added to the blockchain. This resulted in users creating unlimited bitcoins irrespective of the economic restrictions. On August 15th more than 184 billion bitcoins were generated in a transaction. This was one of the most severe of security flaws in Bitcoins history and within hours these transitions were tracked and erased from the logs and the bug was fixed with an updated version of the Bitcoin protocol.

Since bitcoin was open source, this has also contributed to the advent of other crypto currencies. There are several enterprises who have experimented with bitcoins. In January 2011, Electronic Frontier Foundation a non-profit group started accepting bitcoins. Electronic Frontier Foundation, temporarily suspended the use of bitcoins and again resumed using it on May 17, 2013. Around June 2011, Wikileaks and several other organizations started accepting bitcoins for donations.

Lately, Overstock, Expedia, Microsoft, NewEgg.com, Zynga, and Subway (limited locations) are some of the major companies that now accept Bitcoin. Around 2011, several videos and other media print started circulating, thereby triggering the spread of bitcoins. WeUseCoins published its video on March 22nd 2011, which became viral instantly and hit over 6.4 million views.

Bitcoin magazine was founded in September 2011 by Vitalik Buterin. Douglas Feigeson of Bit bills filed a patent application for "Creating and using Digital Currency" on December 23rd 2011. Bitcoin Foundation was launched in September 2012 to accelerate the spread of the Bitcoin protocol. This was launched by Gavin Andresen along with Patrick Murck, Charlie Shrem, Jon Matonis and Peter Vessenes.

Around October 2012, BitPay reported over 1000 merchants accepting bitcoins for payments. WordPress started accepting bitcoins in November

2012. In a single month, February 2013, the bitcoin based payment processor, Coinbase reported selling $1 million worth of bitcoins at over $22 per bitcoin. Around this time, Internet Archive announced accepting bitcoins for donations and also provided options for employees to receive a portion of their salaries in bitcoins.

In March 2013, the blockchain was temporarily split into two different, independent chains with different rules. This halted the bitcoin traffic for almost 6 hours, before the normal operation was restored. This eventually resulted in sell-offs and exchange rates briefly dipped by 23%. During this time frame, Mt.Gox temporarily halted the exchange of bitcoins. Mt.Gox is a Tokyo based bitcoin exchange and catered to more than 70% of all bitcoin transactions worldwide.

This is followed by BitInstant. FinCEN – Financial Crimes Enforcement Network was established in US to introduce regulatory guidelines for decentralized digital currency. According to FinCEN, the bitcoin miners who sell their bitcoins as Money Service

Businesses are subject to registration and other legal obligations.

April 2013, saw a sudden delay in processing capacity at Mt.Gox and BitInstant due to insufficient capacity. This eventually hit the market and dropped the rates from $266 to $76 for 6 hours before returning to $160. Other services such as OkCupid and Foodler began accepting bitcoin payments and eventually led ta greater publicity around bitcoin transactions.

On May 15th 2013, the US seized accounts linked to Mt.Gox since it was not registered as a money transmitter with FinCEN. In July 2013, a project was started in Kenya to link bitcoins with M-Pesa, which is a popular mobile payment system. This was the first initiative to spread bitcoin across Africa. In October 2013 in the FBI seized almost 26,000 BTC from the website Silk Road. This resulted in the arrest of its owner Ross William Ulbricht who worked under pseudonym "Dread Pirate Roberts". Silk Road was an online black market or darknct markct and was notorious for the distribution and sale of illegal drugs. It was part of dark web and was operated as a hidden service. Silk Road 2.0, was brought online on 6th November 2014, however this was also shut down with immediate effect and led to the arrest of the alleged operator.

The world's first Bitcoin ATM was launched on October 29th 2013, by two companies Robocoin and Bitcoiniacs and launched in Vancouver, Canada at a coffee shop. Baidu a Chinese based Internet giant, started accepting bitcoins around November 2013. In November 2013 the largest university in Cyprus, University of Nicosia started accepting bitcoins for payment of tuition fees.

Around November 2013, BTC China, a China based bitcoin exchange overtook Japan based Mt.Gox and Europe based Bitstamp, to become the largest bitcoin trading exchange company. As mentioned earlier, Overstock.com announced plans to accept bitcoin payments in 2014.

On December 5th 2013, Peoples Bank of China, prohibited institutions from using bitcoins for payments. This resulted in the drop of bitcoin exchange rates and eventually Baidu stopped accepting bitcoins for certain services. Bitcoins was tried by several gaming companies around 2014. In January 2014, Zynga announced testing of bitcoins for seven of its games.

In January 2014, The D Las Vegas Casino Hotel and Golden Gate Hotel & Casino started accepting bitcoins. Around this period, the network rate exceeded by 10 petahash/sec. In February 2014, Mt.Gox suspended withdrawals due to technical glitches. In the same month, Mt.Gox announced bankruptcy protection in Japan with reports of 7,44,000 bitcoins being stolen. The network exceeded 100 petahash/sec, in June 2014.

The same year in July, Dell and Newegg started accepting bitcoins. In December Microsoft started accepting bitcoins for Windows software. In January 2015, Coinbase raised 75 million USD, which was the highest for a bitcoin company. Bitstamp a UK based bitcoin exchange, announced to be taken offline owing to 19000 bitcoins being stolen from their hot wallets.

This remained offline for several days before resuming back services on 9th January 2015.

On March 21st, 2015, Inc announced to have raised 116 million USD in venture funding, which is the highest amount for any digital currency related companies. As of August 2015, around 160,000 vendors accepted bitcoins.

Barclays made the announcement to become the first high street bank to start accepting bitcoins and partnered in 2016 with a mobile payment startup – Circle Internet Financial. In October 2015, a proposal was submitted to the Unicode Consortium to add the required code for bitcoin symbol. The network rate exceeded 1 exahash/sec, in January 2016.

The Cabinet of Japan in March 2016 recognized and gave the same status to virtual currencies as real money. South Africa's largest online market place Bidorbuy, launched bitcoin payments for both buyers and sellers. Stream, in April 2016, started accepting bitcoins for video games and other online media. In Argentina, Uber started bitcoin trades after government blocked credit card companies from dealing with Uber. A major bitcoin exchange Bitfinex, was hacked in August 2016. The hack amounted in over 1,20,000 BTC being stolen.

In September 2016 there were around 771 bitcoin ATMs worldwide. In November 2016, SBB – Swiss Railway Operator upgraded all their automated ticket machines to make bitcoin transactions. From the beginning until 2016, bitcoin has attracted several academic enthusiasts. Google Scholar articles published about bitcoin increased from 83 in 2009 to 424 in 2012 and further increased to 3580 in 2016. Also the first edition of academic ledger/journal was published and was edited by Peter Rizun.

In 2017, bitcoin trades have increased exponentially. In January 2017, NHK – Japan, reported that the number of online stores accepting bitcoins in Japan had increased 4.6 times over 2016. BitPay CEO Stephen Pair declared the company's transaction rate grew 3 times between 2016 and 2017. He stated bitcoin as the largest contributor for the sudden increase in the B2B supply chain payments.

The number of Github projects related to bitcoins increased to over 10,000 in March 2017. Bitcoin exchange trading volumes has also seen exponential increases. Mexican exchange Bitso in March 2017, saw a trading volume increase by 1500%. Poloniex, US based digital asset exchange saw an increase of more than 600% active traders and processed 640% more transactions. June 2017, bitcoin symbol was encoded in Unicode 10.0 with code point U+20BF. On August 2017, traditional bitcoin was split into two digital currencies – classic bitcoin which is BTC and Bitcoin cash which is BCH. On November 29th 2017, bitcoin, surpassed $11,000 for the first time.

Altcoins

What are Altcoins? Altcoins is a term used to describe all other cryptocurrencies besides Bitcoin. In other words, alternate coins. Apart from bitcoin, there are several other cryptocurrencies available in the market. There are more than 1000 cryptocurrencies which are available. Some of the most popular ones are – Litecoin, Ethereum, Zcash, Dash, Ripple, Monero, Peercoin, Primecoin, Namecoin, Quark, Freicoin, Mastercoin, Auroracoin. Some of the more popular cryptocurrencies are explained below-

Litecoin – It is a peer to peer virtual currency and is open source. This was created on October 7th 2011 by Charlee Lee a MIT graduate and former Google engineer. Litecoin is similar to bitcoin. The significant difference is the speed of Litecoin. LItecoins are more CPU efficient and the generation rates are faster. It is the first cryptocurrency to use Scrypt as a hashing algorithm.

Similar to Bitcoin, this uses the Proof of Work concept to accept new blocks. The symbol is LTC. The market cap is around $553.3 million. The analogy is, if bitcoin is gold, then Litecoin is silver in the cryptocurrency world. It was released under the MIT/X11 license. Litecoin can handle higher transaction volumes than Bitcoin. Wallet encryption is secure and allows users to view transaction and account balance but requires password before spending Litecoins. Each miner gets a reward of 25 new Litecoins per block and like bitcoin this gets halved every 4 years. The Litecoin blockchain can produce a total of 84 million Litecoins until the reward is reduced to zero. This is almost 4 times the currency units as bitcoins. It is valued roughly around $160.00 as on December 9th, 2017.

Litecoin is one of the top 5 cryptocurrencies. It is aimed to process a block every 2.5 minutes and are more complicated to create as compared to bitcoins.

Ethereum – Ethereum is the second biggest digital currency. Ethereum was first propose by Vitalik Buterin, a programmer and researcher of cryptocurrency. It was fully developed and launched on July 30th 2015 with pre-mined coins of around 11.9 million coins. Ethereum uses Ethash as a cryptography algorithm. The symbol is ETH. It supports Turing complete smart contracts as well as the Proof of Work concept.

Ethereum platform has two versions – Ethereum classic (ETC) and Ethereum (ETH). Ethereum classic provides great opportunities to miners and is presently considered as one of the most profitable tokens to mine. The market cap for Ethereum – ETH is around $448.9 million and the market cap for Ethereum classic is around $294.5 million.

Zcash – Zcash is a project developed out of Zerocoin. Zcash is a decentralized and open source project which was developed in 2016. The founder of Zcash is Zooko Wilcox-O'Hearn. The team consisted cryptographers Matthew D. Green from Johns Hopkins University. Zcash's initial investor includes Roger Ver. Similar to bitcoin, the limit for Zcash is 21 million units.

In the initial 4 years, 20% of the Zcash created was given as the reward to the developers, investors and non-profit organizations. Zcash was formally introduced on October 28th 2016. Zcash provides privacy and transparency to transactions. The analogy is if bitcoin is http, then Zcash is like https. It provides extra security and transparency for every transaction on the blockchain. Details of sender, recipient and amount of transaction remain private.

It also has an option of shielded transaction, which allows content to be encrypted using advanced cryptographic techniques or zero knowledge proof construction called a zk-SNARK. The symbol is ZEC. This uses Equihash for cryptographic algorithm. It is the first open system implementing zero knowledge security. The market cap is around $89.1 million.

Dash – This was originally known as darkcoin. This is a more secretive version of bitcoin. This is similar to bitcoin and forms a decentralized architecture. It offers high level anonymity and the transactions are untraceable. This was launched in January 2014. It was originally released on January 18th 2014 as XCoin (XCO). This name was changed to Darkcoin in February 2014.

It was created and developed by Evan Duffield. This can be mined using CPU or GPU. Darkcoin was rebranded to Dash in March 2015, which stands for digital cash. The rebranding did not alter any of the technical features. Dash acquired several miners within a short period of time and in the first two days of launch almost 1.9 million coins were mined. This is approximately 10% of the coins that will ever be created. In June 2017, the trade volume of Dash had reached $100 million per day. The market cap is around $4.8 billion.

Ripple – Ripple is a real time global settlement network. Ripple offers instant, guaranteed and low cost international payments. This allows smooth cross border payments and provides end to end transparency. This was released in 2012. It has a market capitalization of about $1.26 billion.

Unlike bitcoins and other cryptocurrencies, Ripple does not require mining. Hence saves on CPU computation and can work on minimum network latency. The symbol is XRP. The original authors include - Arthur Britto, David Schwartz, Ryan Fugger. At its core Ripple is a shared, public database or ledger. It is used by companies such as Santander, UniCredit and UBS. It has been widely adopted by banks and payment networks.

Ripple predecessor is Ripplepay which was developed by Ryan Fugger in 2004, who was a web developer in Vancouver, British Columbia. This led to the conception of Ripple by Jed McCaleb of eDonkey network. This was later developed in May 2011 by Arthur Britto and David Schwartz with the help of Ryan Fugger. It is a digital currency system in which transaction are verified by consensus with other network members, unlike the mining process used by bitcoins to add a new block onto the blockchain.

Monero – Monero provides secrecy, privacy and is untraceable. It is also open source cryptocurrency developed in April 2014. This is completely community driven and works on a donation based system. It is decentralized and scalable and works on a special technique called "ring signatures". This means it is impossible to determine which of the group member's keys was used to generate the signature. Monero maintains anonymity of the transaction.

The symbol is XMR. Monero is based on the CryptoNote protocol. It was developed by pseudonymous authors Nicolas van Saberhagen in October 2013. This was originally launched by

Bitcointalk forum and was named as BitMonero and later got renamed as Monero. Market capitalization is around $33.9 million.

Namecoin – It is the first fork of bitcoin. The symbol is NMC. 21 million namecoins are released and are halved every four years. This was developed on 18th April 2011. Similar to bitcoin, it uses the proof of work algorithm. The founder of Namecoin is Vincent Durham. It is decentralized open software system and used SHA-256 algorithm. The market cap is around $3.4 million.

Swiftcoin – It is a cryptocurrency using decentralized and peer to peer architecture. This also uses the proof of work concept. It was developed by Team Daniel Bruno in 2011. It uses similar blockchain technology as bitcoin and is an alternative to bitcoin. This uses SHA-256 algorithm for encryption. Swiftcoins cannot be mined and works on the principal of Solidus Bonds and is not open sourced.

Peercoin - It is also referred as PPCoin or PPC. It is a peer to peer system and uses proof of work along with proof of stake principles. It was developed based on a White paper released in August 2012. The authors include Scott Nadal and Sunny King which are pseudonymous. Sunny King also developed Primecoin.

Peercoin shares much of the code similar to bitcoin and was the concept inspired by bitcoins. It is distributed under MIT/X11 software license and uses SHA – 256 protocol. A peercoin is issued when the hash value is found and the block is added to the blockchain. It is exchanged for fiat currencies, bitcoins and other cryptocurrencies.

Dogecoin - Dogecoin developed its own online community extremely quickly and reached a capitalization of around $60 million in 2014. It was introduced on December 8th 2013. As of November 2017, more than 111 billion coins have been mined. Dogecoin had a very fast initial production schedule as compared to other cryptocurrencies and was created by Billy Markus from Portland, Oregon.

Other well-known cryptocurrencies include – Emercoin, Gridcoin, Omni, Primecoin, Auroracoin,

Blackcoin, and many more. There are well over 1000+ cryptocurrencies in circulation.

Mining explained

I mentioned mining earlier in the book. Below is more explanation on the concept of mining and how it serves as the validation checkpoint which essentially keeps things honest. Bitcoin and other cryptocurrency mining has become very popular in recent years and has gained a lot of attention and resources worldwide. The term "mining" is essentially a metaphor and comparison to when gold was mined. It's comparable because it's a scarce resource, the difficulty rises as there are less gold and more miners, plus there's a reward.

So, you may be asking, what is the purpose of mining and how do people get rewarded? As mentioned the blockchain is a decentralized ledger and is the platform used for people to send or receive transactions...in this case cryptocurrency. These transactions are collected and eventually creates a block, which then gets added to the blockchain.

These cryptocurrency blockchains are essentially created by the miners. These miners are running a piece of software on a computer, originally for Bitcoin.

As the number of people grew who mined, the computers needed had to grow in processing power as well. These days you need specific hardware geared towards mining with extremely powerful GPU's which were originally used for gaming systems. Whether you are mining using a computer or you're using a specialized mining device, you are part of a worldwide network and are volunteering your computer's processing power and electricity which is powering the entire network with everyone else.

Everyone on the network contributes to creating these blocks and if you solve the algorithm, you are rewarded with whichever cryptocurrency being mined. The algorithms and computations are needed to officially publish or add blocks to the chain and are validated through Proof of Work which ensures the integrity and security of that block. It also varies over time since part of the process allowing mining of cryptocurrencies is to have a regulated release of coins. The release of these cryptocurrencies will eventually reach a cap or max coins ever produced.

Again, in the case of Bitcoin, Satoshi Nagamoto programmed the Bitcoin release to have a cap of 21 million total Bitcoins. This will be the max amount of Bitcoins ever released and mined. Nagamoto created in such a way where it is released on a specific schedule and didn't want to create the situation where all the coins were mined in 6 months. The pace of mining is slowed mathematically which increases the difficulty as the number of people mining increase while the number of available Bitcoins decrease.

There a few types of mining. One is where you are mining by yourself and your device mines for whichever currency being sought. If you manage to find and run the correct calculation for the block and successfully add to the blockchain, you are granted the entire reward. It has become very difficult to mine solo, so most people have joined pools of miners. You basically pool your resources together and use what is called a mining pool. Everyone is contributing to creating these blocks and as a result, get rewarded faster. But with that, you are essentially sharing the reward proportionate to the amount of work your system put in.

As a miner, you are part of a decentralized, distributed network and everyone in your pool is volunteering their work and electricity to power the network to allow these transactions and blocks to be created. As a result of all the attention to mining, it has become difficult to mine solo and even part of a pool. The main challenge is the ever increasing difficulty mathematically to solve for blocks, the processing power and more expensive hardware needed, and a huge drain and expense of electricity

As a result, there are now huge warehouses all over the world running massive servers, doing nothing but mining. Some of these are state sponsored in countries like China, Russia, and others. One of the concerns is if there is a specific mining operation that can control over 50% of the network by owning 50+ % of the currency, they have the ability to take down the network. This is avoided by the sheer nature of the blockchain's decentralization and worldwide participation which keeps things fully spread across the network.

Smart contracts

What is a smart contract? It's an agreement online which essentially mirrors any contract you have in real life or physical form. It could be a home, auto, rental, or any countless contracts that we deal with in our lives. Smart contracts basically remove the middle man from executing these contracts.

Typically if you want to go buy a home you go through a process of lawyers, notaries, finance companies, title companies, real estate contracts and it slows down the entire process by having to physically sign, await confirmation, funds clearing – for example. But with smart contracts, you can do that all on your own and secure on the blockchain. Again, you're not going through any central authority, like a bank or auto finance company, or mortgage/title company.

You are facilitating the contract on your own. In an up and running smart contract setup, there would already be a smart contract online. The smart contract, within the blockchain, will have all the details of a regular contract already ready for input. Because you are interacting directly with the person you're transacting with (seller, buyer, tenant, etc), it is much faster, secure, and cheaper. Again, since the blockchain is encrypted and secure, it allows for very complex agreements as all of the details would be pre-programmed and intermediaries or middlemen would not be needed.

Smart contracts provide a real time service which can potentially cut closing times on global from weeks to hours or minutes. Smart contracts can be used for supply chain management as an example. Walmart and IBM are working with China on numerous supply chain contracts, including tracking and ensuring health standards of pork sold in the US as an example.

In summary, a smart contract is an agreement between parties online which can be executed on a transparent, fast, secure blockchain which can include multi-parties, if needed, thus eliminating the middleman which ultimately saves time, money, and ensures accuracy.

Blockchain facts summarized

Bitcoin – a money exchange system pioneered blockchain technology and has more than 8 million accounts. It has grown by more than 100% since it began in 2010.

Blockchain can be public based on internet or private based on intranet

Blockchain is to digital transactions, similar to what internet is to communication. In terms of development, blockchain is what internet was 20 years' back

Only 0.5% of world's population uses blockchain today

IBM and Microsoft are few of the tech giants investing in blockchain

IBM dedicates about $200 million to blockchain powered projects

Financial sectors and banking domains are exploring blockchain options

It is estimated that by using blockchain, the infrastructural costs for driving business, will be reduced by 30%

Smooth and Seamless: Blockchain makes digital transfer of assets between peers extremely seamless. Peer to peer digital transfer is smooth and extremely easy

Security: This uses well-known forms of cryptography to secure information, thereby keeping transactions secure and safe. Works on private key cryptography.

Zero External Dependency: No need to depend on third party agencies to build trust

Decentralized: There is no single point of ownership. Has a decentralized architecture.

Fast Transfer: Since no third party dependency exists, transfer of funds and digital assets can be done almost immediately with no substantial time lags.

Flexible: Blockchains are flexible and can add multiple parties to the existing chain easily

Easy Audits: Maintaining historic audits is possible for every digital asset transaction. Tracing back a transaction details is extremely simple

Cost-effective: Is less expensive for maintenance since no additional infrastructure or additional license costs exists

Performance: Can leverage high speed performance and support quick digital transfers

Expandable: Bitcoin which is digital currency is one of the forms of blockchain. Apart from monetary transfers, blockchain can be visualized and applied for other digital asset transactions. Can be applied to prove your identity.

Data Alteration: Once data is written into blockchain, it cannot be removed or altered. Data is practically not removable by intention.

Popular blockchain systems include-

- BigChainDB
- Chain Core
- Corda

- Credits
- Domus Tower blockchain
- Elements blockchain platform
- Eris
- Ethereum
- HydraChain
- Hyperledger Fabric
- Hyperledger Iroha
- Hyperledger Sawtooth Lake
- Multichain
- Openchain
- Quorum
- StellarSymbiont Assembly

Popular companies exploring blockchain options include- Nestle SA, Ascribe, BitProof, Kroger Co, UProov, Colu, Everledger, Wal-Mart Stores, McCormick & Company Inc, Dole Food Company Inc, Berkshire Hathaway's McLane Co, Filament, Genecoin, Bank of America, Standard Chartered and many more. The list of companies exploring and using blockchain is diverse and continues to grow exponentially.

Closing

I hope this has helped and informed you on the various aspects of blockchains and cryptocurrencies. This technical innovation has been called by some, the Fourth Industrial Revolution. It has inspired many industries to research and innovate and utilize the same technology as was initially implemented. It has also garnered a lot of fear and controversy amongst big institutions as it threatens their livelihood and financial interests.

Smart contracts is the next big set of real life applications where the blockchain is utilized to store contracts. As discussed, the nature of blockchain ensures security, speed, and cost savings. Between blockchain and smart contracts, it enables and empowers individuals. It eliminates the need for central banking institutions whereby you control your money and makes virtually all transactions seamless, secure, fast, and ultimately decentralized.

There is still a lot of work to be done, but since it is open source, it utilizes a worldwide knowledge and skill base of developers which strengthen the technology. I think Bitcoin's value and some other cryptocurrencies show a lot of the same characteristics of the dot com bubble, as most economists say, but the underlying technology of blockchain is where the real money will be made. The worlds' biggest exchange for Bitcoin is Coinbase. Coinbase is based in San Francisco, CA and they have the biggest growth in exchanges due to the ease of getting started. They specialize in offering Bitcoin, Ethereum, and LiteCoin. It is extremely easy to get started by funding with a credit card or your checking account. One myth is that in order to buy Bitcoin, you need to pay for the entire coin. Instead, you can start out with as low as $100 and buy shares of any of the coins offered. Regardless of which cryptocurrency is being traded, one thing is certain: Blockchain technology is here to stay and is potentially the biggest, major market disruptor we will ever see.

Thank you for reading, and again, I hope this book was informative. On a personal note, I want to thank my beautiful wife, Becky, who supported me during this endeavour as I wasn't the easiest to be around during creation of this book 😊

Please continue your research and get involved, Blockchain is here to stay!

Bitcoin Quotes

"I think the internet is going to be one of the major forces for reducing the role of government. The one thing that's missing but that will soon be developed, is a reliable e-cash."- **Professor Milton Friedman, a Nobel Prize winner in economics**

"The swarm is headed towards us" - **Satoshi Nakamoto, when WikiLeaks started accepting Bitcoin donation**

"Bitcoin seems to be a very promising idea. I like the idea of basing security on the assumption that the CPU power of honest participants outweighs that of the attacker. It is a very modern notion that exploits the power of the long tail." - **Hal Finney**

"Bitcoin enables certain uses that are very unique. I think it offers possibilities that no other currency allows. For example the ability to spend a coin that only occurs when two separate parties agree to spend the coin; with a third party that couldn't run away with the coin itself." - **Pieter Wuille**

"Hey, obviously this is a very interesting time to be in Bitcoin center now, but if you guys want to argue over whether this is reality or not, one Bitcoin will feed over 40 homeless people in Pensacola center now. If you guys want proof Bitcoin is real, send them to me, I'll cash them out and feed homeless people." - **Jason King**

"Blockchain is the tech. Bitcoin is merely the first mainstream manifestation of its potential." - **Marc Kenigsberg**

"Bitcoin was created to serve a highly political intent, a free and uncensored network where all can participate with equal access." - **Amir Taaki**

"When I first heard about Bitcoin, I thought it was impossible. How can you have a purely digital currency? Can't I just copy your hard drive and have your bitcoins? I didn't understand how that could be done, and then I looked into it and it was brilliant" - **Jeff Garzik**

"As the value goes up, heads start to swivel and skeptics begin to soften. Starting a new currency is easy, anyone can do it. The trick is getting people to accept it, because it is their use that gives the "money" value." - **Adam B. Levine**

"At its core, bitcoin is a smart currency, designed by very forward-thinking engineers. It eliminates the need for banks, gets rid of credit card fees, currency exchange fees, money transfer fees, and reduces the need for lawyers in transitions1... all good things" - **Peter Diamandis**

"Bitcoin, and the ideas behind it, will be a disrupter to the traditional notions of currency. In the end, currency will be better for it." - **Edmund C. Moy**

"Cryptocurrency Protocols Are Like Onions... One common design philosophy among many cryptocurrency 2.0 protocols is the idea that, just like the internet, cryptocurrency design would work best if protocols split off into different layers. Under this strain of thought, Bitcoin is to be thought of as a sort of TCP/IP of the cryptocurrency ecosystem, and other next-generation protocols can be built on top of Bitcoin much like we have SMTP for email, HTTP for webpages and XMPP for chat all on top of TCP as a common underlying data layer." - **Vitalik Buterin**

"The bitcoin world is this new ecosystem where it doesn't cost that much to start a new bitcoin company, it doesn't cost much to start owning bitcoin either, and it is a much more efficient way of moving money around the world." - **Tim Draper**

"I love seeing new services constantly starting to accept Bitcoin. Bitcoin is really becoming "the currency of the Internet." I'm most concerned by possible government reactions to Bitcoin. They can't destroy Bitcoin, but they could really slow things down by making exchange much more difficult." - **Michael Marquardt**

"Cryptocurrency is such a powerful concept that it can almost overturn governments" - **Charles Lee**

"Economists and journalists often get caught up in this question: Why does Bitcoin have value? And the answer is very easy. Because it is useful and scarce." - **Erik Voorhees**

"I think the fact that within the bitcoin universe an algorithm replaces the functions of [the government] ... is actually pretty cool. I am a big fan of Bitcoin" - **Al Gore, 45th Vice President of the United States**

"I do think Bitcoin is the first [encrypted money] that has the potential to do something like change the world." - **Peter Thiel, Co-Founder of Paypal**

"So bitcoin is cyber snob currency..." - **William Shatner, Actor known for lead role in Star Trek TOS**

"Bitcoin is a remarkable cryptographic achievement and the ability to create something that is not duplicable in the digital world has enormous value" - **Eric Schmidt, CEO of Google**

"Bitcoin is the most important invention in the history of the world since the Internet." - **Roger Ver**

Money is a collective agreement. If enough people come to the same agreement, what they agree upon becomes secondary, whether it be farm animals, gold, diamonds, paper, or simply a code. History proves all these cases to be true. Who knows what the future is going suggest to us as money, once we see digital currencies as ordinary?" - **S.E. Sever, Writer**

I understand the political ramifications of [bitcoin] and I think that government should stay out of them and they should be perfectly legal."
- **Ron Paul, Republican Texas Congressman and former candidate for US President**

"Cryptology represents the future of privacy [and] by implication [it] also represents the future of money, and the future of banking and finance." - **Orlin Grabbe, Economist**

"Gold is a great way to preserve wealth, but it is hard to move around. You do need some kind of alternative and Bitcoin fits the bill. I'm not surprised to see that happening." - **Jim Rickards, American Lawyer, Economist and Investment Banker**

"What can't kill Bitcoin, makes it (us) stronger." - **Mark Wittkowski, Online marketer, coach and pioneer in online lead generation.**

"Bitcoin is a technological tour de force." - **Bill Gates, Microsoft co-founder**

"Every informed person needs to know about Bitcoin because it might be one of the world's most important developments." - **Leon Luow, Nobel Peace prize nominee**

"The relative success of the bitcoin proves that money first and foremost depends on trust. Neither gold nor bonds are needed to back up a currency." - **Arnon Grunberg, Writer**

"The governments of the world have spent hundreds and hundreds of trillions of dollars bailing out a decaying, dickensian, outmoded system called banking, when the solution to the future of finance is peer-to-peer. It's going to be alternative currencies like bitcoin and it's not actually going to be a banking system as we had before 2008." - **Patrick Young, Financial analyst**

"Instant transactions, no waiting for checks to clear, no chargebacks (merchants will like this), no account freezes (look out Paypal), no international wire transfer fee, no fees of any kind, no minimum balance, no maximum balance, worldwide access, always open, no waiting for business hours to make transactions, no waiting for an account to be approved before transacting, open an account in a few seconds, as easy as email, no bank account needed, extremely poor people can use it, extremely wealthy people can use it, no printing press, no hyper-inflation, no debt limit votes, no bank bailouts, completely voluntary. This sounds like the best payment system in the world!" - **Trace Mayer J.D., a Leading Monetary Expert on Bitcoin and Gold**

"You can't stop things like Bitcoin. It will be everywhere and the world will have to readjust. World governments will have to readjust" - **John McAfee, Founder of McAfee**

"It's money 2.0, a huge huge huge deal." - **Chamath Palihapitiya, Previous head of AOL instant messenger**

"We have elected to put our money and faith in a mathematical framework that is free of politics and human error." - **Tyler Winklevoss, Co-creator of Facebook**

"Entire classes of bugs are missing." - **Dan Kaminsky, Security Penetration Expert for Cisco and Avaya**

"There are 3 eras of currency: Commodity based, politically based, and now, math based." - **Chris Dixon, Co-founder of Hunch now owned by Ebay, Co-founder of SiteAdvisor now owned by McAfee**

Bitcoin may be the TCP/IP of money." - **Paul Buchheit, Creator of Gmail**

"I am very intrigued by Bitcoin. It has all the signs. Paradigm shift, hackers love it, yet it's derided as a toy. Just like microcomputers." - **Paul Graham, Creator of Yahoo Store**

"I really like Bitcoin. I own Bitcoins. It's a store of value, a distributed ledger. It's a great place to put assets, especially in places like Argentina with 40 percent inflation, where $1 today is worth 60 cents in a year, and a government's currency does not hold value. It's also a good investment vehicle if you have an appetite for risk. But it won't be a currency until volatility slows down." - **David Marcus, CEO of Paypal**

"[Virtual Currencies] may hold long-term promise, particularly if the innovations promote a faster, more secure and more efficient payment system." - **Ben Bernanke, Chairman of the Federal Reserve**

"Virgin Galactic is a bold entrepreneurial technology. It's driving a revolution and Bitcoin is doing just the same when it comes to inventing a new currency." - **Sir Richard Branson, Founder of Virgin Records, Virgin Galactic, and 400+ other businesses**

"Bitcoin actually has the balance and incentives center, and that is why it is starting to take off" - **Julian Assange, Founder of Wikileaks**

"[Bitcoin] is a very exciting development, it might lead to a world currency. I think over the next decade it will grow to become one of the most important ways to pay for things and transfer assets." - **Kim Dotcom, CEO of MegaUpload**

"At our venture firm, we continue to see an escalating stream of fascinating new Bitcoin uses cases and applications from entrepeneurs." - **Marc Andreessen, Venture Capitalist, Founder of Netscape, Jan 5, 2015**

"Bitcoin, and the ideas behind it, will be a disrupter to the traditional notions of currency. In the end, currency will be better for it." - **Edmund Moy, 38th Director of the United States Mint, May 23, 2014**

"The Federal Reserve simply does not have authority to supervise or regulate bitcoin in any way" - **Janet Yellen, Chair of the US Federal Reserve, Feb 27, 2014**

"Stay away from it. It's a mirage, basically" - **Warren Buffet, CEO of Berkshire Hathaway, Feb 14 2014**

"Bitcoin is evil." - **Paul Krugman, Nobel-prize winning economist, Dec 28, 2013**

Resources

Current market cap:

https://coinmarketcap.com/

Cryptocurrency stats:

https://bitinfocharts.com/

https://www.cryptocompare.com/

Satoshi Nagamoto whitepaper:

https://bitcoin.org/bitcoin.pdf

Cryptocurrency news:

https://www.cryptocoinsnews.com/

Copyright

No part of this eBook may be reproduced or transmitted in any form or by any means, electronic or mechanical, including photocopying, recording or by any information storage and retrieval system, without written permission from the author.

The information provided within this eBook is for general informational purposes only. While we try to keep the information up-to-date and correct, there are no representations or warranties, express or implied, about the completeness, accuracy, reliability, suitability or availability with respect to the information, products, services, or related graphics contained in this eBook for any purpose. Any use of this information is at your own risk.

The methods describe within this eBook are the author's personal thoughts. They are not intended to be a definitive set of instructions for this project. You may discover there are other methods and materials to accomplish the same end result.

- Jim Moran

www.ingramcontent.com/pod-product-compliance
Lightning Source LLC
Chambersburg PA
CBHW040234220526
45473CB00001B/243